"When Kathi McGookey sent me this book to blurb I started reading and just kept going. Though these poems are inventive, they are far more serious as discoveries. I took *Heart in a Jar* literally as I read poem after poem thinking that was exactly what was going on in her head: I can easily see her walking in slow circles around her subjects, stepping closer, looking in to see what makes the world tick. Every poem in this book is like a heart in a jar. Kathi's superb eye and exacting craft rides on the power of images that throttle the reader off the page, yet one foot is so firmly rooted in the real world, we feel incredibly satisfied that we took a wild journey and came back home safely. These poems are a great ticket, existing as tremendous short scripts for the films she directs in our heads."

—Michael Delp,
author of *Lying in the River's Dark Bed*

"McGookey's miniatures are part Alice in Wonderland, part Dance Macabre, and they sing with wisdom—*As for theories*, she writes, *I like luck*. In her quiet looking glass we glimpse worlds as well-constructed as dioramas, both surreal and domestic, a museum of mice eggs, beautiful (sometimes wounded) children, *a crown of tiny pinecones, a tethered owl, mushrooms that rise up like ghost fruit,* a place where *fireflies are strung up and dangle by the glass walls.* When McGookey addresses Death, *Let's pretend you forget all about us,* she stops us in our tracks. This collection charms, ravages, and dazzles."

—Bonnie Jo Campbell,
author of *Mothers Tell Your Daughters*

HEART IN A JAR

Heart in a Jar

Kathleen McGookey

WHITE PINE PRESS / BUFFALO. NEW YORK

White Pine Press
P.O. Box 236
Buffalo, New York 14201

www.whitepine.org

Acknowledgments: These poems appeared, sometimes in different forms, in the following journals. I am grateful to the editors and staffs of each.
"This Was My Real Life," *Artful Dodge*. "Possum Skull in the Field," "Passage," *basalt*. "Thank You for Your Question," "Apology to My Son," *Chariton Review*. "When My Son Goes to Middle School, I Read Audubon," "Today, on Norris Road," *Cloudbank*.
Acknowledgments continue on page 70.

Publication of this book was made possible, in part, by public funds from the New York State Council on the Arts with the support of Governor Andrew M. Cuomo and the New York State Legislature, a State Agency and with funds from the National Endowment for the Arts, which believes that a great nation deserves great art.

Cover image: "Sparrow, Big Sur, 2015" by Elaine LaMattina. Oil on canvas. Used by permission of the artist.

Printed and bound in the United States of America.

ISBN 978-1-945680-02-1

Library of Congress number 2016949217

as always, for Rhys

CONTENTS

Dear Death / 11

Mended II / 12

Folk Tale / 13

Thank You for Your Question / 14

This Was My Real Life / 15

Dear M, / 16

Reasons I Might Understand / 17

Death, Yesterday / 18

Hippopotamus Hide Box / 19

Into the Dollhouse / 20

The Life Below / 21

In My Pink Room / 22

The Secondhand Star /23

Death, Let's Find / 24

At the School Costume Parade / 25

Monkey Island / 26

Tornado Machine / 27

Windfall / 28

In My River / 29

Possum Skull in the Field / 30

Pain Lake / 31

Death, Now Where's the Skinny Stray / 32

Dr. Holtgrieve, DDS / 33

Another Kind of Pain / 34

The Grief Jacket Project / 35

Corrections / 36

Private / 37

Death, Vary Your Question / 38

At the Football Game / 39

Like His Heart in a Jar / 40

When My Son Goes to Middle School, I Read Audubon 41

Pull Up Your Red Pickup / 42

Homesickness / 43

Good Reason / 44

Postcard from a Little Boat / 45

Once / 46

The Zoo in Winter / 47

At the Dance Lesson / 48

The Day After a Girl Sprouted in the Flowerbed / 49

Fairy Tale / 50

The Day's Catch / 51

It's March, Death / 52

Under the Red Umbrella / 53

Illness in October / 54

Sleeping Bear / 55

On the Day of the Dead / 56

Reverence for Life Service / 57

Ordinary Objects, Extraordinary Emotions / 58

Take this Scrap of My Words, / 59

Passage / 60

Lighthouse Tour, South Manitou Island / 61

To Clarify: / 62

Today, on Norris Road / 63

At the John Ball Zoo / 64

At the Zoo, Again / 65

The Long Silence / 66

P.S. Death / 67

Apology to My Son / 68

About the Author / 69

HEART IN A JAR

Dear Death,

can't you see we're busy riding bikes in the sun? Later we'll cut out paper hearts and sprinkle them with glitter. I have had enough of you. I'd rather learn facts about penguins: what they eat, how much they weigh, how they stay warm in the Antarctic. Some are called Emperor. Some, Rockhopper. First-graders with gap-toothed smiles hold out the class guinea pig for me to pet. Let's pretend you forget all about us.

Mended II

I mend what I can. What I can't, I throw away. I wish I were a new tooth, slowly sprouting into a just-cleared space. I don't win every argument. I was once a miracle to my parents. Now I sweep the floor. Is that a miracle, too? My muscles are stiff. I say *I don't know* twenty times some days. I try to protect one boy at the bus stop, the one who gets snowballs thrown at him. I could do a better job. I wonder who might come to my funeral, although I know I should not wonder about a thing like that. I believe the dishwasher swallowed the lost tooth. I am not sure who put the tooth there, but I know it was an accident. I am not sure where my mother and father's love for me has gone, now that they are dead. Today, it feels like the last, brief bit of birdsong, just before the sparrow in the pine flies away.

Folk Tale

I stole the newborn from next door. Then I gobbled him right up, teeny fingernails and all. He curled and shrank inside me, glad for a place like home. His parents, though distraught, soon sank into sleep on the couch, lights still on. Outside their window, I watched them breathe. I watched the moonlight pool in their yard. I wanted to tuck a quilt under their chins: they just needed rest. Though I wouldn't show for weeks, I hoped in nine months they might do the same for me.

Thank You for Your Question

I was unprepared for the sacrifice and noise. What did I know about earwax and antibiotics, carseats, or lost blankets with yellow stars? Caden from preschool had not yet chased my son with the potty plunger. Noah had not yet chewed with his mouth open at snacktime. Freddie had not pinched Carson. Halle had not asked to sit in my lap. To say whether I enjoyed it? I liked rocking in 4 a.m. darkness, sleepy and afraid a face would appear at the window. Or that I'd hear, over the monitor, a stranger in the baby's room. But days full of obvious work, nowhere to be, alone with the baby, I would not have believed.

This Was My Real Life

We lost our house, so we set up a tent. Three tents. The tents sat in dirt. Bugs lived off our blood. Instead of having nothing, I told myself, all this belonged to me: the deep lake, the outhouse, the maple that grew so low over the water we could walk its thick trunk. The one bullfrog in the lake, beneath the tree. Was I parent or child? Both, it seemed, and I was adrift.

A small boy showed us how the pump worked: he threw his weight on the handle until a thin stream gurgled out. He said we had to be strong. So I tried philosophy, imagined I was not the sum of my hauled-away boxes; I was, simply, pure essence. A house offers what protection? Soon I let the children sleep in their clothes. Sometimes we ate. Sometimes we didn't wash for days.

This was our luck: we were too tired to fight. One night I laid my hand on my husband's forehead, afraid of the lightning I saw through my eyelids. Afraid of what my mistakes might mean for us all.

At twilight, no matter the weather, that single bullfrog called to me. Every morning, too. It became familiar: A drum? A heart? Too loud, too slow, too erratic. But still, I wondered if it was mine. Each night, too, when darkness rose up from the ground, animals rustled in the leaves, creeping closer to the tents, then waiting. I brushed my teeth, spit the froth into poison ivy. I let the lamp burn as long as I could. But in the morning, I found the raccoons' greedy dirty footprints on our cooler. We still had, at least, something they wanted.

Dear M,

Having a child is not what you think. Unlike us, even up close, they are perfect. Their pearly skin glows. They are usually born complete: fingernails! eyelashes! mouths that open! I am only guessing you are sad because you do not have one. Yet you still have the beautiful privacy of your mind. You have whole afternoons to watch clouds. Having a child does not help me breathe. Last night I drove halfway to the store with a toddler on my lap before I realized and buckled him into a carseat. Then I drove a schoolbus uphill through a haunted forest. Gray mannequins hung from trees, red mouths open. And I just hoped my daughter in seat five would close her eyes. When I glanced down at the gearshift, I forgot how to drive. I cannot ask the dreams to stop. We have barely met. I write this intending to comfort you.

Sincerely, K

Reasons I Might Understand

I am familiar with snow. With a wrinkled and skinny infant whose arrival was never a sure thing—which isn't the same as a child who never arrives, I know.

I know I am clumsy. Should I begin with artificial dusk, the ultrasound's hum? The room's chill, the hot gel the sonographer rubs on your belly? Or how I imagined, for months, a small boy throwing his arms around my knees? How that ghost-boy made me ache?

I try not to romanticize death. I'll never say my parents can hold your lost baby in heaven, anytime they want. In absence, anyone is perfect. I've learned that the hard way.

Death, Yesterday

my neighbor's boxer, glossy and muscular, charged me again, kicking up dead leaves. This time, it snarled and jammed its open mouth against my calf. I had picked up my daughter and was walking away. It didn't draw blood. So far, you have been more considerate. You don't pick fights. As for theories, I like luck. But each morning, when I hear the white-throated sparrow making its threats at dawn, I know you're not far behind.

Hippopotamus Hide Box

Lock me in the little room with that box. There's no dust. No washing machine or mop. Just mute heads of antelopes and giraffes, whose flat plastic eyes aren't as bad as you'd think. The fireplace never fills with ash. It's cozy in a dollhouse sort of way, even the zebra hair rug. But that hippo hide box is the size of a couch and smells like sun blazing on mud. Whale bones litter the only sky. Fireflies are strung up and dangle by the glass walls. Eventually, someone may notice my absence.

Into the Dollhouse

The pregnant skunk moves into the dollhouse—it is available—then nibbles hard-boiled eggs at the table set for three. My daughter is delighted with her miniature pet, even the muddy stars it left on the stairs. It piles eggshells by its plate. It does not rearrange the furniture or dig up the painted wooden yard. It studies the ABCs. It balances wreaths of silk flowers on its nose. But it dreams of honeybees, sunflower seeds, and oozing, rotten mice. In the kitchen, it backs into cupboards and twitches its tail. It lines the bedroom closet with mud and tufts of black and white fur. Don't look under the bed. It wants a pet of its own. At night, my daughter shines a tiny flashlight through the windows to watch it sleep.

The Life Below

All winter our mice laid eggs under the stairs near the furnace. My parents never mentioned the growing pile that lit the basement with its pearly glow. Grandmother wanted to sell them, but when Mother approached with a basket, our mice reared up and snarled. Snow like feathers covered our little house, covered our broken rakes and sad charred sticks. When I snuck down with apples and walnuts, the mice let me crochet spiderwebs into a necklace for my teacher, a single egg suspended like a jewel. The warm pile stirred and whispered against my back. The furnace ticked and the mice rolled egg after egg under the stairs.

In My Pink Room

I lean into my mirror and it swallows me up. *A real girl!* they yell and rush to touch me, almost sincerely. Feather boas snake around my ankles. A shadowy girl hands me a mask on a stick and some crayons. *Isn't my blood perfect?* I whisper and show her my gouged ankle. Night falls in my pink room. I watch my mother smooth the covers around the doll baby in my bed.

The Secondhand Star

The star was dying, but I bought it anyway from the shop that sold used things. For days it flickered on my bookshelf. Every night when the sun set, it would groan. Some nights it sobbed. The sound was muffled, like the star was politely hiding its head under a pillow. I liked its light, which changed from yellow to pink on my bedroom walls, but its whimpers and hiccups entered my dreams. Each morning I woke groggy with sadness. I couldn't push the star back into the sky because it had grown heavier as its light dimmed. My brother could have it if he could take it away. Together we rolled it out the window and into the flowerbed, where it landed near the rhododendrons. It made a soft sound like air rushing out the valve of a bicycle tire. For weeks the star glimmered down there, silent. Winter came and my parents locked my window. I hardly thought of the star covered in snow. When I slept, I dreamed it had begun to whisper urgently, and I wanted to hear what it might say.

Death, Let's Find

a rock that looks like an egg so some other mouth can tell me about possibility. What do you know about the bruise that's just bloomed over my eye? I've no memory of injury. Wasn't it yesterday the tethered owl nuzzled her keeper's finger and the keeper told us, *Put your hands in your pockets*. Weren't we in line behind two children holding cloth-covered baskets of chicks? I thought you'd join me occasionally when the weather was fine, to walk through sunlight and road dust, and then past the swamp. My mistake.

At the School Costume Parade

Sadness fills me and I can't give it back. A sleek bee sting and gauzy kisses won't help. Octopus, vampire, cowgirl, bat. Smear flour on a bruised cheek, tooth-marked, and now you're a zombie. Now Death dangles a plane in the sky. A ladybug trips over a desk and wails. Swollen tentacles sweep cupcakes to the floor. I feel like crying. I'd take the dark forest over the crowd in here, where the werewolf needs his sticky scruff adjusted. And what's more, the bride doesn't intend to marry him. I want to bend down and whisper, *My darlings, smiling exhausts me.*

Monkey Island

The monkeys inside me are sick of speaking the wrong language. One rides a red bicycle in circles. Another wonders if she is flawed because what she reads does not make her weep. When lightning startles them awake, they eat bananas and wait for the houses to open their eyes. The third monkey always chooses the front seat of the automatic train that zooms through Copenhagen: it's best for spotting new graffiti. The last monkey wants to swim for it. She believes the vast ocean is only a trick of the eye.

Tornado Machine

Dorothy orders the tabletop model. Emerald green. Finally, a way to send the gifts she has gathered into Oz: fountain pen, rare prairie wildflowers in bloom, bulletproof vest. She pushes the button. Vapors swirl and gather, then a tiny funnel cloud rises, a ghost tornado. Sometimes the connection falters, and the mist crashes and settles into soft waves. She runs her hand right through it and doesn't feel a thing, mist trailing her pinkie.

The turbo setting is a huge improvement, but it sucks up a tea towel and apple pie before she can switch it off. Only a note, then. She decides to risk *Heart, brain and courage working well? Love from Kansas, Dorothy.* The words will surely arrive as confetti. It pains her to send her friends the possibility of *rage* and *rain,* but in the worst case, she reasons, they could still spell out *They love my art.*

Windfall

When our angel arrived hungry, wearing a crown of tiny pinecones, Mother threw open our doors. Who knew when luck might smile a little on us again? Our angel promised to scrub floors, but we got down on our knees anyway, our hearts like rabbits. After she mended our sugar bowl, she kissed each cube she tossed back in. We gave her the bed near the window, a fancy book of paper dolls. Now the peaches in our orchard throb like little bombs. The dolls grew wings and the whole flock buzzes as she fills her basket with windfall. When they land on our ears and shoulders, when they tangle in our hair, Mother shoos them away. Our mouths are dry. Mother whispers, *Behave yourselves!* and shoves us forward. Behind her, skunks and snakes, doves and mice, crowd each other. Mushrooms rise up like ghost fruit rotting under the trees.

In My River

We sleep in wet beds and hear our mothers calling us. We have always lived this way. Our teeth are white and sharp and long as the bones of fish. When the moon shines in my river, when a butterfly tries to lay eggs on it, we must not touch. The doctor had said, *This won't hurt*, before she pulled clocks and feathers from the incisions she'd made in our sides. We'd believed her, once. The butterfly turns its dark eyes toward us, its wings tattered and damp. Its eggs glow pink and pale blue with speckles. They drift and swirl. It is raining, just barely, and the rain feels like the sleek fur of otters against our cheeks. Our mothers call and call for us. In one egg, we find a garland. In another, worn-out ballet shoes. In the last, a doll whose head is the skull of a mouse.

Possum Skull in the Field

Divine Spirit, let the large thing with claws have finished me quickly. Day has come; I am lying in its light. Let the light come again and again. I am safe now in any weather. Let the barn owl coast above me; let the worms come. Let skin and blood and muscle fade. Let a wren take fur for its nest, to warm five speckled eggs. Let the nestlings fly. I never was anything but pure and stupid ache. Let sunset paint my bones the color of roses. Give me, finally, a boy with dirty hands. He will not see my stained and broken teeth, he will not notice half my jaw is gone. Let him shout and run for his father, let them exclaim over what I have carried within me that has risen up, what has carried me. Let them carry me home like an egg made of glass.

Pain Lake

Dive in, leave yours behind. Or just dip your toe. Afterward, you can sit and watch the sky bleed. Someone will hand you a dandelion bouquet and a glass of water. Someone will braid your hair. The wooden sign by the water is faded now. If the wind kicks up, you can chase beach balls with the kids and dogs who splash by the reeds. Yes, they feel it. More than you'd think. It is unfortunate or not, depending.

Death, Now Where's the Skinny Stray

that's already killed a finch and a robin? She's littered feathers like petals in the yard. For three days, she followed us to the bus stop, but she vanished when I prepared a box. Did you know I planned to drive that cozy box to the shelter? Did you know I told my kids, *There's a chance this cat will find a home.* I know truth is precarious. And here you've sent a curtain of rain for the cat to hide behind. In winter, I imagined, she would starve and freeze. In summer, she watches with you...

Dr. Holtgrieve, DDS

Dr. Holtgrieve, Dr. don't-grieve, Dr. hold-your-grieving holds a wet
cloth to my forehead. When the fillings hurt my teeth, he ground
them out and drilled them in again, no charge. He says to his assis-
tant, *She's getting some color back.* When he talked surgery, he said *snip.*
He said *quick.* He said *Nothing to worry about. Any questions?* He never
says *blood.* He says: *Assistant, rinse.* He says, *Bite down. We've got to stop the
flow.* Dr. don't-grieve-for-me tips me back and kittens stare down
from the ceiling. They are all trust. Dr. Holtgrieve washes his hands
where I can see. He holds the door open and says, *You should heal in
a week. Take it easy.*

Another Kind of Pain

Our parents gave us Christmas checks for $27.42 or $15.78 along
with our gifts. My brother said to the minister, *They'd saw a penny in
half if they could,* and she repeated this at their funeral. Fair, sure.
Scrupulous. I'd always cut the chocolate cake and my brother would
choose the first slice. So when our dog was run over, when our friend
drowned the day his brother won the spelling bee—this was another
kind of pain. Or was it growing up?

Now, one of us parks a black BMW in the garage. The other one is
woken by a toddler who says, *Please want me.*

The Grief Jacket Project

Admittedly, the project's nature—to develop a wearable jacket that physically protects and comforts mourners—led the committee to make impractical suggestions. One member wanted letters from her beloved screened onto a lining of China silk. Another requested fabric knitted with yarn spun from the milky green and gold chrysalis of a monarch butterfly. Our first prototype, a long-sleeved canvas coat lined with mink and entirely covered with small, smooth river rocks, was primitive, and its sheer weight discouraged elderly widows from trying it. The engineers among us then turned to sea turtle shells, seeking to improve ease of movement by crocheting the scutes together. Testers, however, said that a fractured shell, though re-attached, offered no coziness and only minimal protection. When a pair of barn swallows swooped by our conference room's windows, the committee rejoiced. Volunteers who tried the final model—sanitized swallow feathers hand-stitched to spandex and lined with milkweed floss—reported feeling jaunty, sleeker than they had thought possible, cheerful, and—inexplicably—hungry. Some sat for hours and petted the sleeves. Each would be delighted to own such a beautiful and useful garment, to be passed down to loved ones when the time came.

Corrections

Let's get a few more things straight: the cat knocked over the water
dish and the large dark circle spread. I will write any address with
immaculate clockwork, immaculate desire, because being an animal
is not so bad, there are whole hours, whole afternoons, to drowse
by the pond in the cornfield. I really do mean animal, not animal
desire, near the dark and expressive eye of the pond. One cannot
look away. I, for one, have a sense of decency and intend to make
these corrections known. I'm preparing a small private room where
not one person's dreams will be allowed to wander.

Private

My dreams say, *Keep the show private.* They do not like to be discussed.
They drip into my head through my ear. Not like poison. But, yes,
like Shakespeare: four lovers, feasting, have eyes only for the person
sitting to their right. They cannot see the soft glances and pretty
words are not for them. The jester rings the bell in the tower but
forgets to release the rope. His skinny green-stockinged legs knock
over the wine. Resolution? A drunk man walks to his house on the
bay. It is morning. He pulls up the wooden blinds. The dawn is not
brilliant, not yellow or white. Impossible. What has he orchestrated?
Are the lovers still unsatisfied? My dreams toss me scraps: a silver
goblet, an enchanted ring, a mumbled phrase about—I think—be-
trayal and revenge. They wink.

Death, Vary Your Question

a little. Inside me are candy stars and cardboard hearts. What's the point in saying you can't have them? Willows, ferns, and river birches still grow beside that pond you dug for me. In here, it's always night. The rooster sleeps all the time. My yellow life raft is covered in ivy now. But if you hold the candle, we can still go for a ride. Push my library receipts out of the way. I like to drift by the brown horse that grazes in a field lit by dandelions. And please look down into the water. I've spent days teaching the paper fish to swim.

At the Football Game

We dash under the bleachers, away from our parents, then trip down a tunnel of dirt. Falling is not so bad: Gabe reaches for the quarters and gum wrappers that tumble with us. We make faces and let the wind fill our cheeks like a couple of fat goldfish. Time stretches out its long beach towel and tells us the water is fine. Then we land with a jolt. Voices can't reach us anymore; we hear roars and silence, alternating like surf, with the muffled cadence of the fight song in between. We have fallen a long way. Gabe holds out a plastic spoon. It's pretty safe down here: no strangers, no drug dealers, no teenagers making out. But we could really use a rope.

Like His Heart in a Jar

The dead cat, stolen from Biology, showed up in my locker. Black-haired Joe, who wanted to be my boyfriend, who sometimes gave me rides in his father's Cadillac, put it there. You'd think it would have been terrible, skinny toad-colored thing dangling from my coat hook, but it didn't stink or drip. After Calculus, it was gone.

When My Son Goes to Middle School, I Read Audubon

Sometimes he can't open his locker. Sometimes the math teacher singles him out. Each day is a sizzling trill, soft sounds like a stake being driven into the ground, a variety of wails, the highest possible violin note. After school, my boy searches through his collection of bird suits: pine siskin, least bittern, brown thrasher, wood thrush. From his closet's messy nest he pulls chimney swift, shakes twigs from its pockets, slips it on. Now he'll ride his silver bicycle until he rises with the clear whistle of wings.

Pull Up Your Red Pickup

to school, Death, it's time for Mrs. Keizer's class party. If you haven't brought Valentines for everyone, you may not pass them out. But you're welcome to braid a friendship bracelet and balance an Oreo on your forehead. Cupcakes go next to the juice boxes. Even with the windows open, the room gets hot. And you should compliment the other moms about their children. No fair watching the moon grow distinct in February's bare sky. Surely you've noticed some child's dead-on free throws or skill with sharp objects? It's ok if you don't exactly fit in. No one wants to believe you are here.

Homesickness

The angel on the bridge in Paris wears his best black suit, his sleekest black wings. Behind him, a lion lies on the concrete, an indifferent royal pet. But the lion does not belong to the angel. Each carefully pretends he is alone. The lion sizes up an iron lamppost. The angel empties his pockets—matchbooks, receipts, foil chocolate wrappers—into the rapidly moving water. I want you to notice the sky, how its creamy yellow is radiant with possibility, like the glow of an unripe peach. Beneficent. Nearly the color of the lightest fur on the lion's muzzle. Of course it's summer, and two people about to fall in love lick ice cream under the bridge, just out of the angel's sight. They've spotted the lion and think he looks tired but kind, willing to give advice.

Good Reason

Someone has already said the night is a ripped tapestry, a tangle of rich shreds. Someone has scribbled all over it. I say the summer night draped over us into the soft wet lap of the waves. The darkness trembled. The expanse of lake trembled, available. I hadn't been to Paris yet. I was going. I was going to return, heavy with the scent of butter melting. I was taken by surprise, taken to the catacombs, its walls inlaid with skulls and bones, miles of intricate patterns, a tourist attraction of unnamed dead, scattered. Yes, taken. As soon as I opened my mouth, I marked myself as *not of this place*. So I had to have good reason.

Postcard from a Little Boat

Friend, I've called no one beloved, not even you. But, yes, in your quiet courtyard off the boulevard, next to a chipped angel, a fountain murmured. A motorcycle pulled up to the cathedral and someone hopped off. Waves of lit votives flickered by the saints inside. Back then, I could have become anyone. Now, let's say my heart is a little boat on a still pond. Let's say papers fall from my hands. Let's say the clock blinking red all night long is nothing like a candle: the wind's wings have knocked out the power again.

Once

I'd like to talk about something else for a change, like that small blue frog, which, if licked, kills whatever licked it. The frog might be another color. You might have to eat it to die. But I know I've got the killing part right. Once, I had patience. Once, I had my own room. I didn't have sisters. I didn't have roosters. I'd like to know who said *I have wasted my life*. And was it true? When I lay my head upon my desk, something inside me—a shadow, a ghost?—tries to sit up. Its outline washes through me, like certain medications. I like not discussing certain subjects. I like going to the orchard to pick fresh peaches. I like the idea of a different life. But that's what I thought years ago, imagining this one.

The Zoo in Winter

suits you, Death. Admission is free. The outdoor tank where jellyfish drifted, luminous, to piped-in Vivaldi, is in storage now. Here's some molasses and nutmeg for the animals' Christmas tree. Which do you like best: eagles under netting-covered sky or steelhead with fraying fins in cloudy water? Or the mountain lion pacing its enclosure's high concrete ledge? Or me, steering my daughter out of the gift shop and into the reptile house? Don't bother saying pain is a necessary teacher. Just look at all your students.

At the Dance Lesson

My teacher says I have springs in my legs. Then we practice skipping, chins up, and I crash through the ceiling. *Yoo-hoo,* Miss Michelle calls from below, *Give that advanced class a try.* Up here, big girls twirl pink hula hoops around their necks. I shake oak splinters from my hair. My new teacher opens a window so light blue clouds slip in. We boogie-woogie, stomp and clap as snowflakes glitter and drift to the floor. I do not fall. I am big enough and good at counting. My breath makes a daisy, a pale feather, a smoky snakeskin. Somewhere, my mother is waiting for me. I fill an icy mirror with my grin.

The Day After a Girl Sprouted in the Flowerbed

Mother yanked her out. I filled my watering can with milk. In the hollow, we could barely see my bedroom's yellow eye. I patted dirt over her bloody roots and stood her up again. When I stroked her cheek, she turned toward me and opened her mouth. And when she sang, she sang about a sparrow and a leaf. And when she yawned, I saw baby teeth. Would she grow? Would she live? She needed a collar of feathers, a pillow of violets. A birchbark suit. A firefly lantern outside a small house made of stones polished in the creek. Mother's shadow opened my window and called. We didn't have long. The tree frogs' silver chorus rose in waves as I ran back to my house. I could still hear the girl's faint sparrow song. Maybe she was calling me.

Fairy Tale

Offer me a peach and a fork. Offer my sadness a small box. Red or gold or white, it doesn't matter. Please don't touch the lit candles on the tree. Store the box until I want it, then tell me a story, the one where I'm happy as a trout because no one catches me. The trout wants a box to call its own. The red fox wants to swim across the river. The bear ran away from the woodsman, then fell asleep in the honey tree. If only we had a brand new axe! Open my box, and you'll find my brand new child. I've been wanting the two of you to meet.

The Day's Catch

A fat and silent baby trembled among the glistening trout when my
husband hauled in the day's catch. We had so much to teach him:
cabbage, crescent, apple, scar. Before he grew much, he blew soapy
kisses at me. I sewed him a cape to wear when the trees swayed. I
glued his wooden turtle back together. On his walls, I painted steel-
head and perch—schools of eyes to watch over him. While I hung
paper hearts in his doorway, the sound of his breathing filled me.
That sound was sweet. That sweetness seeped into the house like
mist and clung to us. The barred owl called and called its story to
someone else each night. When that baby cried, his tears wove a wet
necklace around me. The stars and moon carried on their tea party
in whispers. And the sunrise arrived late as usual, spilling tangerines
all over the dirty dishes in my sink.

It's March, Death

and why do my frostbitten daffodils want to see this world again?
Talking to you feeds my illusion of control. On a scale of one to
ten, please rate your feelings about spring. Without it, you're stuck
in your room, where you could reorganize your collection of teeth.
Or sharpen a few pencils. Or shake up your snow globe, the little
one, the one you pretend to see the future in, the one with the golden
Buddha inside.

Under the Red Umbrella

Once I read in a children's book that rain never changes, that the rain on our roof and windows also fell on the dinosaurs. I liked this idea. It comforted me: the same rain—constant soundtrack—on everything, on whatever came first and next and next, on Socrates and Shakespeare and Einstein, then eventually on me in France, waiting to be kissed.

The next time I miss my mother, maybe I'll go out in the rain. We must have walked in it many times under the red umbrella with the broken handle, maybe waiting for my school bus, holding hands or not, laughing or not, standing close, then closer, because we wanted to stay dry.

Illness in October

A photograph, black and white, of hands clasping. Two people lean against each other. Sorrow stuns itself against the window. Cat banished, then sought. Forget the weather. Forget the rotting vines, the garden's wet-leaf muck. Is that the steady breath of a sleeper? Is that a clock's bald wet face in the mirror?

Sleeping Bear

I climb the dune's highest hill. I want to fly away home. Up here, it's quiet and breezy. Slowly, a toy boat draws a white line across Glen Lake. My heart calms. The people who climb after me have not hurt each other. Campers stream off a blue school bus, then wobble in canoes near shore. Though I know they must be singing, I can't hear the song.

On the Day of the Dead

I wait like an egg for you. You do not come through the field, boots wet and dark. You do not crouch in the dusk or the mist that rises to the horizon. I've unlocked my window and put on my red scarf. I've wrapped up my nightmare and left it by the door. Here's a candle. Here's a sandwich. Here's your antique dresser in the garage, drawers jammed with photos and silver trays. What do you make of it? What do you make of me now? Your journey can't be easy. Let your fingers grow eyes, let all those eyes fill with tears. I am flying a bright flock of kites so you can find your way back to me.

Reverence for Life Service

My boy carried his cat's picture and small tin of ashes to church. Others brought living pets. We lined up and the minister said a special prayer for our dead cat. One bright fish circled in its bowl on the altar. Sick of crying, I cried again. When we sang *For the Beauty of the Earth*, the words were different than the ones I sang when I was young.

Ordinary Objects, Extraordinary Emotions

Dear Kathleen McGookey, Thank you for submitting your deceased mother's eyeglasses, straw fishing hat she wore as a child, and vial of four wisdom teeth for the Grand Rapids Public Museum's juried Day of the Dead exhibition "Ordinary Objects, Extraordinary Emotions." We carefully examined your loved one's belongings, but found they weren't quite what we were looking for. We received 7,562 items, with eyeglasses, hearing aids, dentures, and pipes topping the list. In fact, we considered commissioning an installation composed entirely of these articles, but as most people wanted their property returned, logistics overwhelmed us. While the selection committee sympathizes with the universal plight of how to dispose of emotionally charged artifacts, we regret we cannot take them into our collection, even temporarily. However, we wanted you to know your materials made it to the final round of consideration and the committee read your cover letter with interest. When they learned you still have your mother's blonde braids, cut off when she was twelve, her blue strapless prom dress, and perfect plaster reproductions of her feet, made when she was fitted for orthopedic shoes, the committee felt you did not submit your best objects. We are returning them in the postage-paid mailer you provided, and we wish you the best of luck placing them elsewhere.

Take This Scrap of My Words,

Death, and fold it into your pocket, snug over your hip. The three white feathers from my pillow smell like my lemon perfume. Don't worry that your pocket has a hole. This time of year, swallows dive for feathers to line their nests. And after it cartwheels over the daffodils, the scrap will land in the gravel. A sparrow will snatch it up. Now what will you remember me by?

Passage

Behind this door, my daughter says, *Remember my kisses.* The August moon, red crescent, sinks into dark trees. What is my most favorite, magical number? Number of steps up the Arc de Triomphe? Number of whitewashed doors, dazzling the San Torini sun? That Greek island never cared about me. Here is the first lost tooth, its wet journey already done. Here are the silver keys to the car. And here is the monarch's chrysalis, dangling under our threshold. Rain and wind worry us, but if we rescue it, we will damage it beyond any repair.

Lighthouse Tour, South Manitou Island

Lake Michigan heaves its slow heartbeat on the sand. The tower narrows the higher we go. My son stomps on each lattice metal step and sand from his shoes sifts through. The tour guide stops our group on each progressively smaller landing, asks, *What part of this lighthouse was built first?* and, after we've climbed through a trapdoor that disappears into floor, *What happened in this room?* I don't lean in or look down. My daughter tugs her braids and asks for my camera. The guide offers a story: here, two older brothers watched their parents' boat go down in a storm. A little light, extinguished, while the lighthouse blinked *I'm here.* At the top, we are allowed outside. *It'll be windy,* the guide says, *so take off your hats.* I glimpse a thin railing and reach for my children. *If you drop anything,* the guide says, *just let it fall.*

To Clarify:

The red flutter on Shaw Lake Road could have been a fallen leaf. Still, I didn't swerve. There are so many. . . .. I know that's the wrong attitude. So far, that's all. So far, so good. When I pick up a dead swallowtail, it's already swarming with ants. So my girl stomps on a cursive ribbon of tar the road crew just laid down. She wants to leave a mark.

Today, on Norris Road

I lifted a painted lady, then a black swallowtail, from the dirt. Each was still a little alive. Each did not want to leave my hand for the dead leaves and tall grasses in the ditch. I am tired of missing you. Let's not wait for the kingdom of heaven to see each other again. On my way home, I walked in the U-shaped prints horses had left in the sand. I told myself it was for luck.

At the John Ball Zoo

Nothing sings or swings or swims in me. No flashing trout, no penguin, no saucy chimpanzee. No bright otter, too smart to be caged. Not one blade of grass. The brown bear cowers when the beverage cart goes by. The curly-horned sheep totters on its concrete cliffs. When will I say, *Grief, I am done with you.* The tiger hasn't moved all morning, then gets to its feet and vomits. When will I say, *Grief, do you miss me, too?*

At the Zoo, Again

Look at that beautiful bear, a woman says. The bear paces and paces a small cement ledge, then stands still, looks out with unfocused, deep-set eyes. My daughter waves and I feel sadder still. I can't explain it's not a pet.

The otter is better: It runs over the rocks, then dives. Silver bubbles cling to its back behind the aquarium window. A girl shakes a leafy branch, the otter chases it, the children laugh and run after. A black-haired toddler wants to see; he wants me to lift him. I'd spotted him earlier, by the tiger, strapped into a stroller. His spiked hair matched his dad's; his sad eyes matched the bear's. I hadn't noticed his fingers were fused into flippers. Now, he smiles at me with his whole face. He raises his arms to me again. I move to lift him but suddenly his mother appears and thanks me, and I haven't done anything.

The Long Silence

When I told my children they could no longer speak, immediately they closed their mouths. They wanted to ask how long, and I wanted to say years, but I showed them the window where the mountain hid in fog. I held out a fossil they'd pulled from the creek. Soon it snowed. Years did pass. In that long silence, I washed dishes. I peeled beets. We forgot we had ever spoken and what we had spoken about. Folding their clothes was like saying prayers. I set out bowls of soup, and while the children ate, a forest rose up. Spiders spun silver hammocks where the children swayed, petting pearl-colored kittens that had dropped from the trees. If they fought, they rolled their eyes and pinched each other and then their fights were done. My daughter sewed dresses of leaves. Green snakes curled around my son's shoulders if he napped outside. When he woke, he built cage after cage of twigs. Soon hundreds of parrots flew in front of the sun, then circled and landed in the trees. They were hungry and lonely. They had traveled a long way to reach us. And then they opened their mouths.

P.S. Death

Lucy just handed me a crumpled page—crayoned numbers orbiting Venus and Mars. The first grade finished their unit on space and started infinity. Our frail neighbor died today, the one who used to watch her swim. Are you chilly up there in your ratty robe and slippers? Lucy would offer you crackers and juice, then lead you to the monkey bars. You'd have fun. But I don't want you to feel at home here.

Apology to My Son

Leave me alone. I want to watch the morning sun turn the tall grass in the field to ash. I want four fat mourning doves to strut the roof's peak, then scatter when a hawk dives. My heart has fetched the stick so many times it does not feel like my heart anymore. Let's cover it with glitter and hang it in the dollhouse. The family who lives there won't mind.

Kathleen McGookey's work has appeared in journals including *Agni, The Antioch Review, Boston Review, Crazyhorse, Denver Quarterly, Epoch, Field, Great River Review, Hunger Mountain, Indiana Review, The Laurel Review, Ploughshares, The Prose Poem: An International Journal, Prairie Schooner, Quarterly West, Seneca Review, Upstreet, West Branch,* and *Willow Springs.* Her work has been nominated for a Pushcart Prize, as well as featured on Poetry Daily and Verse Daily. The author of *Whatever Shines, October Again,* and *Mended,* she is also the translator of *We'll See,* prose poems by French writer Georges Godeau. McGookey's book *Stay* was published by Press 53 in 2015. She has received grants from the French Ministry of Foreign Affairs, the Irving S. Gilmore Foundation, the Arts Fund of Kalamazoo County, and the Sustainable Arts Foundation. After earning her MFA and PhD from Western Michigan University, she taught creative writing at Hope College, Interlochen Arts Academy, and Western Michigan University, as well as in private workshops. She lives in Middleville, Michigan, with her family.

Author photograph: Kaitlin LaMoine Martin

Acknowledgments, continued from copyright page

"Dear Death," "Death, Now Where's the Skinny Stray" (as "Hide and Seek"), "P.S. Death," *Columbia Poetry Review.* "Monkey Island," *Crazyhorse.* "Windfall," *Dash.* "Illness in October" (as "October, Illness"), *Diode.* "In My Pink Room," *dislocate.* "Lighthouse Tour, South Manitou Island," *Dunes Review.* "Reasons I Might Understand," *Encore.* "At the Dance Lesson," *5 AM. Magazine,* "The Day After a Girl Sprouted in the Flowerbed," *Four Way Review.* "Take This Scrap of My Words," *Glassworks.* "Pain Lake," "Like His Heart in a Jar," *The Great River Review.* "Under the Red Umbrella," *Hotel Amerika.* "Fairy Tale," "Tornado Machine," *The Literary Review.* "Corrections," *Meridian.* "Ordinary Objects, Extraordinary Emotions," *MiPoesias.* "Death, Yesterday," "It's March, Death," "Reverence for Life Service," *Miramar.* "At the School Costume Parade," *New Delta Review.* "In My River," "The Life Below," *Ninth Letter.* "Dear M," *Prairie Schooner.* "Sleeping Bear," "At the Zoo, Again," "Into the Dollhouse," *The Prose-Poem Project.* "The Day's Catch," *Quiddity.* "Postcard from a Little Boat," "At the John Ball Zoo," "On the Day of the Dead" (as "I Wait,") *Rhino.* "Private," *Sentence.* "Folk Tale," *SLAB.* "Death, Let's Find," "Death, Vary Your Question" (as "Vary your question a little…,") *Sugar House Review.* "The Zoo in Winter," *Upstreet.* "Homesickness," "Once" as ("I'd Like to Talk About Something Else"), *Wake: Great Lakes Thought & Culture.* "The Long Silence," *Waterstone Review.* "The Secondhand Star," *Waxwing.*

"Dear Death," "Death, Yesterday," "Pull Up Your Red Pickup," "Death, Now Where's the Skinny Stray," "P.S., Death," and "Take This Scrap of My Words" appear in *Nothing to Declare: A Guide to the Flash Sequence,* published by White Pine Press.

"At the John Ball Zoo" and "Fairy Tale" appear in my chapbook *October Again,* published by Burnside Review Press and reprinted by the Friends of Poetry.

"Tornado Machine," "Mended II," "Thank You for Your Question," "Possum Skull in the Field," "Dear Death," "Pain Lake," "Home-sickness," "Postcard from a Little Boat," "I Wait," "Sleeping Bear," "To Clarify:," "Like Stars," and "Passage" appear in my chapbook *Mended*, published by Kattywompus Press.

"Sleeping Bear" was first published as a limited-edition broadside by The Michigan Poet. It also appears in the anthologies *Poetry in Michigan / Michigan in Poetry* (New Issues Press, 2013) and *The Michigan Poet Collected Poems 2010-2016* (The Michigan Poet, 2016).

"The Long Silence" appears in the anthology *Borderlands and Cross-roads: Writing the Motherland* (Demeter Press).

"Passage" first appeared as a limited-edition chapbook illustrated by Yolanda Gonzalez and published by the Urban Institute for Contemporary Arts in Grand Rapids, Michigan.

"Today on Norris Road" was a part of the "Sense of Place" exhibit at the Portage District Library, in Portage, Michigan. Artist Nina Feirer created the gorgeous quilt "Autumn Leaving" in response to my poem.

So many people have helped shape my poems and this manuscript. Thank you to Jane Hilberry for her beautiful poem "She Keeps Her Heart," which inspired this book's title; I am indebted to Bonnie Jo Campbell and Susan Ramsey for that brilliant suggestion. Thank you to my writing groups, both in person and online. I am especially grateful to Nin Andrews, Priscilla Atkins, Margaret DeRitter, Elizabeth Kerlikowske, Gail Martin, Jack Ridl, and Julie Stotz-Ghosh. I send my deep gratitude to Dennis Maloney and Elaine LaMattina of White Pine Press for taking such wonderful care of my poems and giving them a home. Thank you to Gary Young for believing in my work. Thank you to Caroline and Tony Grant of the Sustainable Arts Foundation for supporting my work. Most of all, to Rhys and Charlie and Lucy: Thank you for everything.